toys to knit

toys to knit

Tracy Chapman

POTTER
CRAFT

NEW YORK

I dedicate this book to my mum

Published in the United States by Potter Craft,
an imprint of the Crown Publishing Group,
a division of Random House, Inc., New York.
www.crownpublishing.com
www.clarksonpotter.com

POTTER CRAFT and CLARKSON N. POTTER are trademarks
and POTTER and colophon are registered trademarks of
Random House, Inc.

Originally published in 2005 in Great Britain
by Collins & Brown Ltd.

Library of Congress Cataloging-in-Publication Data is
available.

ISBN 0-307-33659-X

Printed in China

Design by Gemma Wilson and Penny Stock
Photography by Mark Winwood
(except pages 2–3, 88–89 and back cover by John Garland)

10 9 8 7 6 5 4 3 2 1

First American Edition

Safety Note
Do not use small beads or buttons on toys intended for use
by babies or children under three years old, as they may cause
a choking hazard if swallowed. Even safety eyes are not
completely safe when used with knitted toys.

Contents

Introduction 6

Dolls 8

Clothes 12

Animals 36

Nursery toys and accessories 74

Yarn Suppliers 92

Useful addresses and suppliers 93

Knitting abbreviations 94

Acknowledgments 96

Introduction

Childhood is a magical time in all our lives and should be captured and treasured. The collection that is *Toys to Knit* is a culmination of many years of research and memories.

I am very fortunate that some of my earliest recollections are of knitting. We would have day trips to the homes of my aunts only to find them rummaging excitedly through their huge stocks of yarn, deciding on what to make next!

My first lessons in knitting were from my mom, who still knits to this day and who has helped me enormously with this book. She patiently taught me the craft and my earliest projects included toys and dolls' clothes. From that moment I was hooked! I'd help Mom sew up and stuff the various very beautiful toys that she made for the local fête, and I'd proudly carry them in my own handmade bag. I would spend all my free time knitting, and collecting yarns, needles, and patterns—which I still do to this day.

Toys to Knit is a collection of my very own special memories: a basic doll that has many guises, an elephant to cuddle, and nursery toys just the right size for tiny hands to hold.

The collection is ideal for anyone with little ones in their life and, of course, a must for anyone who loves the innocent appeal of wooly characters. The projects will make wonderful gifts for babies, toddlers, and children who are just learning about life.

Happy knitting!

Dolls

This section of the book gives you the pattern for the Basic Doll, which can be adapted to make other dolls. Once you have mastered the simple pattern on pages 10–11, you can experiment with different facial expressions and hairstyles to create your own cast of characters. There's also a whole wardrobe of patterns for a closet full of doll's clothes. Make tutus, leg warmers, sweaters, hats, little shoes, and other darling accessories to keep your dolls well outfitted for any occasion.

Basic doll

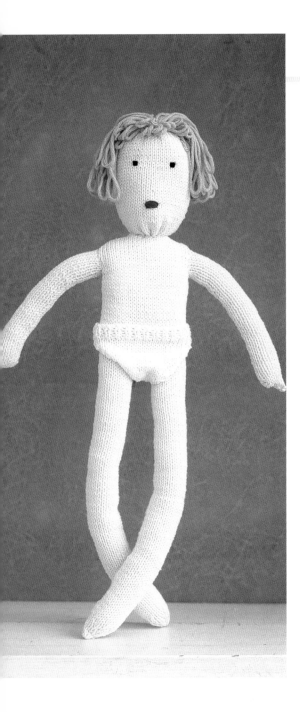

Use the Basic Doll pattern as your foundation for a whole family of dolls. Turn to page 13 for a selection of clothes to suit her every mood and social engagement, or make her into any of the variations that appear later on in the book.

MATERIALS

- **Fingering yarn:**
  2 oz. pale pink
  2 oz. light brown
  2 oz. white
- Black and pink embroidery thread for eyes and mouth
- Needles: size 2–3
- Toy stuffing

For all main body pieces, use pale pink.

HEAD
Cast on 21 sts.
1st row: K.
2nd row: K1, inc in next st, P to last stitch, inc in next st, k1 (23 sts).
3rd row: K.
4th row: As row 2 (25 sts).
5th row: K.
6th row: K1, P to last st, k1.
Continue in stocking stitch, without further shaping, for 32 rows.
Next row: K2tog twelve times, k1 (13 sts).
Next row: P.
Next row: K2tog six times, k1 (6 sts).
Bind off.
Make another piece to match.

LEGS
Cast on 24 sts.
Stocking stitch 64 rows.
Decrease as follows:
Next row: K1,* k2tog, k2, rep from * to last 3 sts, k2tog, k1 (18 sts).
Next row: P.
Next row: K1, *k2tog, k2, rep from * to last 1 st, k1 (11 sts).
Next row: P.
Next row: K1, * k2tog, k2, rep from * to last 1 st, k1.
Next row: P.
Next row: K1, * k2tog, k2, rep from * to last 2 sts, k2 (9 sts).
Next row: P.
Break thread and draw through remaining 9 sts and secure. Make another leg.

BODY

Cast on 28 sts.
Stocking stitch for 36 rows.
Bind off 4 sts at the beg of next 4 rows (12 sts).
Bind off remaining 12 sts.
Make another piece the same.

ARMS

Cast on 16 sts.
Stocking stitch 50 rows.
Bind off 4 sts at beg of next 4 rows.
Make another arm.

TO MAKE UP BASIC DOLL

Sew in all ends. Join head pieces, using mattress stitch, and stuff firmly. Join the two body pieces in the same way and stuff. Join seams of legs, stuff firmly and attach to bottom of body. Fold and close seams on arms. Attach to main body. Attach head to complete the doll, ensuring that the neck is stuffed sufficiently to support it.

HAIR

To make the hair, begin at the back of neck: sew a loop, then secure with a small stitch. Continue working in this manner until whole head is covered. Make the bangs in the same way, using shorter loops.

FEATURES

Sew features on the face as illustrated, using black embroidery thread for the eyes and pink for the lips.

PANTIES

Use white.
Cast on 24 sts.
Work in k1 p1 rib for 4 rows.
Stocking stitch 4 rows.
Next row: Dec 1 st at each end of next and every following alt row until 10 sts rem.
Next row: K2tog to end (5 sts).
Stocking stitch 3 rows.
Next row: Inc in every st (10 sts).
Next row: Inc 1 st at each end of next and every following alt row until there are 24 sts.
Stocking stitch 4 rows.
Work in k1 p1 rib for 4 rows.
Bind off.
Fold in half and join the side seams.

Clothes

**Here you'll find a range of outfits to dress the
Basic Doll in:** she has a fashionable collection of
everyday clothes, but you may also wish to experiment
with various colors and yarns to extend her wardrobe—
doesn't every doll deserve to have a closet that is
bursting at the seams?

There are also special costumes to transform the Basic
Doll into a ballerina, a sailor, an ethereal fairy, a striking
Japanese girl, or a lovable rag doll.

Basic wardrobe

The Basic Doll has a set of mix and match outfits to choose from: a wrap top, a pretty skirt with a motif around the hem, a Fair Isle sweater with a snowflake pattern, a pair of snug pants, a jacket, hat, and shoes. Knit her the whole set and she'll always look perfectly turned out—and ready for any adventure.

Wrap top

MATERIALS
- **Fingering yarn:**
  2 oz. purple
- **Needles:** size 2–3

Cast on 28 sts.
Stocking stitch 28 rows.
Next row: K9, bind off center 10 sts and K to end.
Working on these 9 sts only, work 2 rows in stocking stitch.
Next row: K1, P to last 1 st, k1.
Next row: K1, pick up loop before next stitch and knit into back of it; knit to end (19 sts).
Continue increasing in this manner on the front edge until there are 28 sts.
Work 1 row.
Next row (RS facing): Cast on 31 sts and K to the end.
Bind off.
With wrong side of work facing, rejoin yarn to remaining sts using stocking stitch. Work 1 row.
Next row: K1, P to last stitch, k1.
Next row: K to last stitch, pick up loop before stitch and K into the back of it, k1.
Repeat the last two rows and continue increasing in this manner, on the front edge only, until there are 28 sts.
Complete to match first side.
Bind off.

SLEEVES
Cast on 22 sts.
Work 6 rows in stocking stitch.
Next row: Increase 1 st at each end of this and following 4th row, until there are 26 sts.
Work 27 rows in stocking stitch.
Bind off.
Make another sleeve to match.

TO MAKE UP WRAP TOP
Fold sleeves in half lengthwise and sew in place on top of shoulder. Join sleeve and side seams.

Striped panties

MATERIALS
- **Fingering yarn:**
  2 oz. purple
  2 oz. white
- **Needles:** size 2–3

The panties are worked in stripes, beginning with the purple. Change color on every third row. Follow instructions for Panties on page 11.

Skirt

MATERIALS
- **Fingering yarn:**
  2 oz. lilac (A)
  2 oz. white (B)
- **Needles:** size 3
- **Small button**

Using main yarn, cast on 140 sts.

Garter stitch (every row knit) for 4 rows.
Stocking stitch 2 rows.
Next row: Using the Fair Isle technique, set motif as illustrated in chart, using contrast yarn.
Continue in stocking stitch for a further 24 rows.
Decrease row.
Next row: K2, * k2tog, repeat from * to last 2 sts, k2 (68 sts).
Next row: P.
Next row: K4, * k2tog, k1,

repeat from * to last 4 sts, k4 (48 sts).
Stocking stitch 2 rows.
Bind off.

TO MAKE UP SKIRT
Darn in all ends on the skirt and join sides with mattress stitch. Leave approx. 1½ in. open at the top. Sew on a small button and crochet a chain to use as a loop.

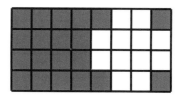

■ A
☐ B

Fair Isle sweater

MATERIALS
● **Worsted yarn:**
   2 oz. cream (A)
   2 oz. light blue (B)
● Needles: size 7

FRONT
Cast on 25 sts.
Work k1 p1 rib for 4 rows.

Continue in stocking stitch for 4 rows.
Next row: Set snowflake motif using Fair Isle technique and following chart on page 17.
K6, next 13 sts follow chart, k6. Work 13-row chart to complete motif.
Continue in main shade only, working a further 4 rows in stocking stitch.
Work 4 rows in k1 p1 rib.
Bind off.

BACK
Work as front, omitting motif.

SLEEVES
Cast on 22 sts.
Work 6 rows in stocking stitch.
Next row: Decrease 1 st at each end of this and every following 4th row until there are 14 sts.
Work 1 row without shaping.
Next row: Work 4 rows of k1 p1 rib.
Bind off.
Make another sleeve to match.

TO MAKE UP THE FAIR ISLE SWEATER
As for Teddy Bear's Blue Sweater (see page 49).

Pants

MATERIALS

- **Worsted yarn:**
  2 oz. light blue
- Needles: size 7
- Elastic: 8 in.

Cast on 25 sts.
Knit 2 rows.
Next row: Beginning with a knit row, work in stocking stitch for 50 rows.

Next row: Work 4 rows in k1 p1 rib. Bind off.
Make another piece to match.

TO MAKE UP PANTS

Darn in all loose ends. Starting at bottom of leg, join seams using mattress stitch. Work until 1½ in. from rib. Join both legs at center seam. Sew elastic around top of pants to form a waistband.

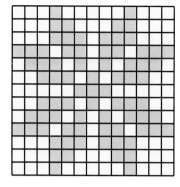

☐ A
☐ B

Ballerina clothes

This graceful ballerina has all the right accessories to use in her exciting performances—a tutu, ballet shoes, leg warmers, and even a delicate necklace!

MATERIALS

- **Fingering yarn:**
  2 oz. brown
  2 oz. dark pink
  2 oz. white
- White worsted remnants for leg warmers
- Needles: size 2–3
- Crochet hook: size C2–D3
- Ballet net: ¼ yd. in either light pink or white
- Bias binding to match net
- Press studs
- 2 sequins, 2 beads, embroidery cotton

HAIR
As Basic Doll. Use brown.

PANTIES
As Basic Doll. Use white.

WRAP TOP
As Wrap Top, on page 14. Use dark pink.

TUTU
Fold the ballet net in half lengthwise and gently gather it to fit around the waist of the doll. Baste as you go, then sew securely. Take the bias binding and fold it over the gathered waist edge of the net. Pin and sew in place, covering the basting stitches. To finish, sew the press stud parts to either end of the waistband. Trim the tutu to the desired length.

SHOES
Use dark pink.
Using the crochet hook, make a foundation ring of 8 ch, join with a slip stitch and work in rounds.
Round 1: Make 2 ch; work 8tr into ring, working over loose end.
Round 2: As round 1.
Round 3: As round 1.
Continue working in this way until shoe fits securely on the foot.
To finish, crochet two chains on either side of shoe to use as straps.
Make another shoe to match.

NECKLACE
Thread two sequins, in different colors and shapes, onto a piece of embroidery cotton. Thread on a bead, then thread the cotton back through the two sequins.

LEG WARMERS
Use white worsted remnants.
Cast on 24 sts.
Continue in k2 p2 rib for 40 rows.
Bind off in pattern.
Make another leg warmer to match.
To finish, join side seams using mattress stitch.

HAIRBAND
Use dark pink.
The hairband is made by casting on 5 sts, and working in stocking stitch until when the hairband is slighty stretched, it fits across the top of the head.

Sailor clothes

Watching the ships in a busy harbor inspired me to design this cheeky chap, full of tall tales about his journeys around the world and encounters with monsters of the deep.

MATERIALS
- **Worsted yarn:**
  2 oz. navy
  2 oz. white
- Needles: size 2–3
- Elastic: ¼ yd.

TUNIC TOP
Use navy.

BACK
Cast on 28 sts.
Stocking stitch until 5½ in long.
Bind off.

FRONT
Cast on 28 sts.
Stocking stitch 26 rows.
Divide for neck: k14, work on these stitches only.
Next row: P.
Decrease 1 st on neck edge on this and following 7 alternate rows (6 sts).
Stocking stitch 3 rows.
Bind off.
Rejoin yarn to remaining 14 sts and reverse shaping to match first side.

TUNIC INSET
Use navy and white.
Using white, cast on 20 sts.
Work in stocking stitch throughout.
Work 11 rows.
Change to navy and K 1 row.
Bind off.

SLEEVES
Use navy.
Cast on 22 sts.
Work 6 rows in stocking stitch.
Next row: Increase 1 st at each end of this and every following 4th row, until there are 26 sts.
Stocking stitch 20 rows.
Bind off.
Make a second sleeve.

PANTS
Use navy.
Cast on 35 sts.
Work 2 rows in garter stitch (every row knit).
Stocking stitch 74 rows.
Next row: K4, * yfwd k2tog, repeat from * four times, K to end of row.
P 2 rows.

Bind off.
Make another piece the same.

COLLAR
Use navy and white.
Using navy, cast on 48 sts.
Work 4 rows in garter stitch.
Change to white yarn.
Next row: K2tog tbl, k12, k2tog tbl, k16, k2tog, k12, k2tog (44 sts).
Row 6: K2tog, K to the last 2 sts, k2tog (42 sts).
Row 7: Rejoin navy, k2tog tbl, k10, k2tog tbl, k14, k2tog, k10, k2tog (38 sts).
Row 8: As row 6 (36 sts).
Row 9: Rejoin white, k2tog tbl, k8, k2tog tbl, k12, k2tog, k8, k2tog (32 sts).
Row 10: As row 6 (30 sts).
Break off white yarn and continue in navy throughout.
Row 11: K2tog tbl, k6, k2tog tbl, k10, k2tog, k6, k2tog (26 sts).
Row 12: K2tog, P to last 2 sts, k2tog (24 sts).
Row 13: K2tog tbl, k4, k2tog tbl, k8, k2tog, k4, k2tog

(20 sts).
Row 14: As row 12 (18 sts).
Row 15: K2tog tbl, k2, k2tog tbl, k6, k2tog, k2, k2tog (14 sts).
Row 16: As row 12 (12 sts).
Bind off.

HAT
Use navy.
Cast on 32 sts.
Work 3 rows in garter stitch.
Row 4: Change to white. Sl1, P to the last st, k1.
Work 2 rows in garter stitch.
Row 7: Sl1, k2, * increase once in the next st, k4, repeat from * to the last 4 sts. Increase once in the next st, k3 (38 sts).

Row 8 (and every following alternate row): Sl1, P to the last st, k1.
Row 9: Sl1, k2, * increase once in the next st, k5, repeat from * to the last 5 sts. Increase once in the next st, k4 (44 sts).
Row 11: Sl1, (k5, k2tog) six times, k1 (38 sts).
Row 13: Sl1, K to the end of the row.
Row 15: Sl1, (k4, k2tog) six times, k1 (32 sts).
Row 17: Sl1, (k3, k2tog) six times, k1 (26 sts).
Row 19: Sl1, (k2, k2tog) six times, k1 (20 sts).
Row 21: Sl1, (k1, k2tog) six times, k1 (14 sts).

Row 23: Sl1, (k2tog) six times, k1 (8 sts).
Break off yarn and draw through remaining stitches and fasten off.

TO MAKE UP SAILOR'S CLOTHES
Darn in all ends. Join seam on hat and stitch open side. Join shoulders on tunic, sew inset into position as illustrated, attach sleeves and sew side and sleeve seams using mattress stitch. Make a twisted cord and thread through eyelets. Starting at bottom of leg, join seams of pants using mattress stitch. Work until 1½ in. from rib. Join both legs at center seam. Thread needle with elastic and sew a length around top of pants to form a waistband.

Fairy clothes

Share magical times with this enchanting fairy. She has very long legs, delicate wings and a beautiful organza skirt that looks like gossamer.

MATERIALS
- **Fingering yarn:**
  2 oz. white
- **Worsted yarn:**
  2 oz. gold
- Needles: size 2–3; size 3
- Crochet hook: size D3
- White organza: ½ yd.
- Bias binding tape: ½ yd.
- Narrow silver ribbon: 1 yd.
- Pins, needle and thread
- Press stud
- 2 buttons

LEGS
To make a long-legged fairy, make legs of Basic Doll as follows: stocking stitch 84 rows (not 64 rows).

HAIR
As Basic Doll. Use gold, doubled.

PANTIES
As Basic Doll. Use white and size 2–3 needles.

TOP
As Sailor's Tunic Top, front sections. Use white and size 3 needles.

The top is constructed by joining the front sections on one side, using mattress stitch. This will be the back seam. Fold the outside edges into the middle and catch the shoulders together to form a jacket. Sew on the buttons, and crochet two small button loops.

WINGS
Use white and size 2–3 needles.
Cast on 42 sts.
Working in garter stitch throughout (every row knit), work 36 rows.
Eyelet row: K2, * yfwd, k2tog, repeat from * to last 2 sts, k2. This forms the holes for the ribbon to be threaded through.

Continue in garter stitch for a further 18 rows.
Bind off.
Thread ribbon through the eyelet holes, pull to gather slightly and tie ribbon around doll's waist to form wings.

SKIRT
Fold the white organza along the width, forming a long rectangle, and baste along the top using running stitch. Gather the fabric to fit around the waist of the fairy and sew securely. Sandwich the raw edge of the organza in between the bias binding tape and pin, baste, and sew in place. Attach the press stud. Trim off any loose threads. Wrap small sections of ribbon around the ankles and sew in place.

Japanese clothes

This pretty girl from the Far East wears a brightly colored traditional kimono and has an upswept hairstyle, decorated with blossoms. Her calm, meditative air makes her a good friend to have around, and she's the perfect confidante. She'll be a welcome guest in anyone's home.

MATERIALS
- **Fingering yarn:**
  2 oz. white
  4 oz. red
  2 oz. light blue
- **Worsted yarn:**
  2 oz. gray
- Needles: size 2–3
- Ribbon: ½ yd. of light blue
- Roses: 3 x mini ribbon roses

HAIR
As Basic Doll. Use gray.
Follow instructions for long hair sections on Rag Doll, using the same technique, but only around the outer hairline. When completed, gather up at crown of head and secure with same yarn. Allow the loose ends to fall equally around the tied hair and gather up to form a bun. Sew securely and attach a rose on the side of the head at the front.

KIMONO
Use red.

BACK
Cast on 34 sts.
K 2 rows.
Next row: K.
Next row: K2, P to last 2 sts, k2.
Repeat the last two rows until work measures 6 in.
Continue in stocking stitch, knitting the first two and last two stitches of every row *
until work measures 10½ in. from cast-on.

SHAPE SHOULDERS
Bind off 6 sts at beginning of next 4 rows (10 sts).
Bind off remaining 10 sts.

FRONT
Work as back until * (8½ in.).
Divide for front.
K17, turn work, k1, P to last st, k1.
Continue on these 17 sts only,
until work measures 10½ in. from cast-on.
Bind off 6 sts (11 sts).
Work 1 row.
Bind off 6 sts (5 sts).
Bind off remaining 5 sts.
Rejoin yarn to remaining 17 sts and work to match first side.

SLEEVES
Cast on 44 sts.
Work 6 rows in garter stitch.
Continue in stocking stitch until work measures 3½ in.
Bind off.
Make another sleeve to match.

TO MAKE UP KIMONO
Darn in all loose ends. Join shoulder seams using mattress stitch. Attach sleeves and join sleeve and side seams. Press work to keep the open side seams flat.

PANTIES
As Basic Doll. Use white.

BACK PILLOW

Use light blue.

Cast on 25 sts.

Work 25 rows in stocking stitch.

Next row (RS): P 1 row—to make fold.

Next row (WS): Continue in stocking stitch, starting with a purl row, and work 24 rows. Bind off.

TO MAKE UP THE BACK PILLOW

Darn in all loose ends. Fold in half and sew sides using mattress stitch. Stuff slightly and close last side. Attach ribbon and roses to pad as illustrated.

Rag doll clothes

With her distinctive golden braids and bubbly bangs, Rag Doll cuts a tall, striking figure. She's happy to sit dangling her long legs over a shelf, watching everything that's going on. She's all ready for summer days in a cute sleeveless top and skirt with interesting hem detail, embellished with an embroidered daisy.

MATERIALS

- **Fingering yarn:**
  2 oz. white
- **Worsted yarn:**
  2 oz. yellow
  2 oz. pink
  2 oz. lilac
- Needles: size 2–3, size 7
- Crochet hook: size D3
- Beads

LEGS

To make a long-legged rag doll, make legs of Basic Doll as follows: stocking stitch 84 rows (not 64 rows).

HAIR

As Basic Doll. Use yellow. To make bangs, follow instructions for Basic Doll. To make the longer sections of hair, cut lengths of yarn measuring 23½ in. and fold in half. Using a crochet hook and starting at the back of the bangs, insert hook and draw

through folded end of yarn; secure by threading long ends through. Tighten up. Repeat this technique in rows across

the head, working down toward the neck. To make braids, divide the hair into two halves and secure

gently. Tidy up both sections and divide each of them into three equal bunches. Braid down the length. Tie with yarn in a bow.

PANTIES
As Basic Doll. Use white and size 2–3 needles.

SKIRT
Use pink and size 7 needles.
Cast on 74 sts.
K 1 row.
Commence pattern:
1st row: K.
2nd row: P.
3rd row: K1, * (k2tog) three times, (yfwd, k1) six times, repeat from * to last st, k1.
4th row: K.
Repeat these 4 rows once more.
With WS facing, work a further 28 rows without shaping.
Next row: K2tog to end of row (37 sts).
Work a further 6 rows in garter stitch.
Bind off.

TO MAKE UP THE SKIRT
Darn in all loose ends and

embroider a 'lazy daisy' motif on bottom of skirt above the pattern sequence.

SLEEVELESS TOP
Use lilac and size 7 needles.

BACK
Using lilac, cast on 25 sts.
Work 4 rows in moss stitch.
Work a further 32 rows in stocking stitch.
Bind off.

FRONT
Using lilac, cast on 25 sts.
Work 4 rows in moss stitch.
Work a further 14 rows in stocking stitch.
Next row: Divide for front.
K13, turn work and P to end.
Next row: K to last 2 sts, k2, turn work and P to end.
Work a further 2 rows without shaping.
Next row: Decrease 1 st at neck edge.
Repeat the last 3 rows until 8 sts remain.
Bind off.
Rejoin yarn to remaining 12 sts and complete to match first side.

TO MAKE UP THE TOP
Darn in all loose ends. Join all seams using mattress stitch. Join shoulder and side seams.

Eskimo Jacket

This beautiful, hooded eskimo jacket can be teamed with a pair of pants or a skirt—perfect when there's a chill in the air.

MATERIALS

- **Fingering yarn:**
  2 oz. fawn
  2 oz. cream
- Needles: size 7

ML—On the right side of the work, knit to the position of the loop. Knit the next stitch, but do not allow the loop to drop off the left-hand needle. Bring the yarn to the front between the two needles and wind the yarn around your left thumb.

Take the yarn to the back again, between the needles, and knit into the same stitch remaining on the left-hand needle—so making two stitches out of the original one. Slip the stitch off the left-hand needle.

Place both stitches back on the left-hand needle and knit them together through the back of the loops to complete the stitch.

MAIN BODY & SLEEVES

(Worked in one piece.)
Use fawn.
Starting at lower edge of back, cast on 26 sts.
Work 16 rows in stocking stitch.

SLEEVE SHAPING

With RS facing and working in stocking stitch throughout, cast on 3 sts at the beg of the next 8 rows (50 sts).
Work 8 rows without further shaping.

NECK SHAPING

K21, cast off center 8 sts, K to end.
Working on first set of 21 sts only and beg with a purl row, stocking stitch 7 rows.
Next row (RS) (neck edge): Cast on 4 sts and K to end (25 sts).
Next row (WS): Bind off 3 sts at sleeve edge on next and three following alt rows (13 sts).
Next row (RS): Beginning with a knit row, work 16 rows in stocking stitch.
Bind off.
With WS facing, rejoin yarn to remaining 21 sts.
Beginning with a purl row, work 6 rows in stocking stitch.
Next row (WS) (neck edge): Cast on 4 sts and purl to end.
Next row (RS): Bind off 3 sts at sleeve edge on the next and three following alt rows (13 sts).
Next row (WS): Beginning with a purl row, work 16 rows in stocking stitch.
Bind off.

HOOD

Use cream.
Cast on 43 sts.
1st row: K1, * ML, k1, rep from * to end.
2nd row: P.
3rd row: As 1st row.
4th row: Change to fawn and purl.
Next row (RS): Beginning with a knit row, continue in stocking stitch until work

measures 2½ in. from cast-on.
Bind off.

TO MAKE UP JACKET
Darn in all loose ends. Fold
hood in half with loops at the
front, join back seam (cast-off
edge) with mattress stitch.
Attach to main body of jacket,
easing the side edges around
neck shaping. Starting a cuff,
join sleeve seams in the same
manner, leaving a 1 in. vent at
the bottom of the side edges.

Make two twisted cords, each
measuring 6 in., and attach to
jacket at the bottom of the
hood on the neck edge.

Floppy brimmed hat

This gorgeous floppy hat is perfect for a lazy day in the sunshine. It can be knitted in any colour to go with the outfit you make for any of the dolls in the book. Here it is modeled by the ballerina doll, but it could work equally well on the rag doll or the basic dolly on page 14.

MATERIALS
- **Worsted yarn:**
  2 oz. cream
- Needles: size 7

CROWN
Cast on 40 sts.
Work 6 rows in stocking stitch.
Shape crown.
7th row: * (K6, k2tog), rep from * to end (35 sts).
8th row: P.
9th row: * (K5, k2tog), rep from * to end (30 sts).
10th row: P.
11th row: * (K4, k2tog), rep from * to end (25 sts).
12th row: P.
13th row: * (K3, k2tog), rep from * to end (20 sts).
14th row: P.
15th row: * (K2, k2tog), rep from * to end (15 sts).
16th row: P.
17th row: * (K1, k2tog), rep from * to end (10 sts).
18th row: P.
Break yarn and draw through remaining 10 sts and secure.

BRIM
With RS facing, pick up and knit 40 sts along cast-on edge of crown.
2nd row (WS): Inc in every stitch (80 sts).
3rd row (RS): * K3, inc 1, rep from * to end (100 sts).
4th row: P.
5th row: K.
6th row: P.
7th row: * K4, inc 1, rep from * to end (120 sts).
8th row: P.
9th row: K.
10th row: P.
11th row (eyelet row): K2, * yfwd, k2tog, rep from * to end.
12th row: P.
13th row: K.
14th row: P.
Bind off.

TO MAKE UP HAT
Darn in all loose ends.
To complete frilly edge, fold along eyelet row and slipstitch into place.
Join seam using mattress stitch.

Boys button-up shoes

MATERIALS
- **Fingering yarn:**
  2 oz. dark denim
- Needles: size 2–3
- 4 small buttons

Cast on 28 sts.
Work 4 rows in single rib, * k1, p1, rep from * to end.
Next row (RS): Work a further 6 rows in garter stitch (every row knit).
Decrease as follows:
11th row: K3, *k2tog, k2, rep from * to last st, k1 (22 sts).
12th row: K.
13th row: K2, *k2tog, k2, rep from * to end (17 sts).
14th row: K.
15th row: K1, * k2tog, k2, rep from * to end (13 sts).
16th row: K.
17th row: K1, * k2tog, rep from * to end (7 sts).
Break yarn, draw through tightly and secure.
Make another shoe to match.

TO MAKE UP SHOES
Darn in all loose ends. Join rib by backstitching, and main panel by picking up stitches from either side and securing.

With seam at the back, sew two buttons onto the front of each shoe as illustrated.

Girl's lace-up shoes

MATERIALS
- **Fingering yarn:**
  2 oz. muted pink
  Remnants of light blue
- Needles: size 2–3
- Crochet hook: size D3

Cast on 28 sts.
Work 2 rows in garter stitch (every row knit).
Next row (eyelet row): K1, * yfwd, k2tog, rep from * to last st, k1.
Next row (WS): K.
Next row (RS): Beginning with a knit row, work 6 rows in stocking stitch.
Decrease as follows:
11th row (RS): K3, * k2 tog, k2, rep from * to last stitch, k1 (22 sts).
12th row: P.
13th row: K2, *k2tog, k2, rep from * to end (17 sts).
14th row: P.
15th row: K1, * k2tog, k2, rep from * to end (13 sts).
16th row: P.
17th row: K1, * k2tog, rep from * to end (7 sts).
Break yarn, draw through tightly and secure.
Make another shoe to match.

SHOELACES
Using crochet hook and oddment of yarn, chain 8½ in. and fasten off.
Make another shoelace to match.

TO MAKE UP SHOES
Darn in all loose ends. Join seams using mattress stitch. With seam at the back, begin in the center front and thread the shoelaces through the row of eyelets. Tie in a bow.

Animals

Each of the animals in this section will make a great gift, which will put a grin on the face of any child or adult. Take a look at cheeky Tucker the Monkey, and Penguin, who has traveled all the way from the Arctic. Who could resist Kangaroo and Baby Roo? Nobody will ever forget Loulou the Elephant. And Reggie the Snake will slither effortlessly into your affections. Each has its own character and style.

Tucker the monkey

This appealing little monkey, with a heart-shaped face, is full of charm. He's curious about life and dressed for adventure in a snazzy vest and scarf. Tucker is full of mischief and great fun to have around.

MATERIALS

- **Worsted yarn:**
  8 oz. brown
  2 oz. fawn
  2 oz. red
  2 oz. green
- Black embroidery thread for eyes, nose and mouth
- Needles: size 2–3
- Double-pointed needles:
  2 x size 2–3
- Toy stuffing

* Yarn to be used doubled (apart from ears)

BODY—BACK

Use brown.
Using the yarn doubled, cast on 12 sts.
Work 2 rows in stocking stitch.
Next row: Increase 1 st at each end of this and every following 4th row until there are 20 sts.
Work 26 rows without shaping.

SHAPE TOP OF BODY BACK

Decrease 1 st at each end of next and every following alt row until there are 6 sts.
Work 1 row.
Bind off.

BODY—FRONT (2 PIECES)

Use brown.

SIDE 1

Using the yarn doubled, cast on 6 sts.
Work 2 rows in stocking stitch.
Next row: Increase 1 st at each end of this and every following 4th row until there are 12 sts.
Work 26 rows without further shaping **.
Next row: With RS facing, decrease 1 st at END of next row and at the END of every following 4th row until there are 8 sts.
Work 1 row.
Next row: Decrease 1 st at each end of this and every following alt row until 2 sts remain.

Bind off.

SIDE 2

Work as side 1 until **.
Decrease at BEGINNING of next row and at the BEGINNING of every following 4th row until there are 8 sts.
Work 1 row.
Next row: Decrease 1 st at each end of this and every following alt row until there are 2 sts.
Bind off.

LEGS

Use brown.
Using the yarn doubled, cast on 20 sts.
Work in stocking stitch, continuing until work measures 8in. (approx. 70 rows).
Bind off.
Make another leg to match.

ARMS

Use brown.
Using the yarn doubled, cast on 16 sts.

Work in stocking stitch, continuing until work measures 6¼in. (approx. 56 rows).

SHAPE TOP OF ARM
K1, k2tog, k4, k2tog, k4, k2tog, k1 (13 sts).
Purl.
K1, k2tog, k7, k2tog, k1 (11 sts).
Purl.
K1, k2tog, k1, k3tog, k1, k2tog, k1 (7 sts).

Purl.
K1, k2tog, k1, k2tog, k1 (5 sts).
Purl.
Bind off.
Make another arm to match.

HEAD
Use brown.
Using the yarn doubled, cast on 9 sts.
Work 2 rows in stocking stitch.
Next row: Increase 1 st at each end of this and every following

alt row until there are 21 sts.
Work a further 20 rows without shaping.
Next row: Decrease 1 st at each end of this and every following row until there are 9 sts.
Bind off.
Make another piece to match.

TAIL
Use brown, using the yarn doubled.
Follow pattern for Mousie Mousie – Tail (see page 00).
Work until it measures 13½in.

HANDS AND FEET—2 PIECES FOR EACH
Use fawn.
Cast on 20 sts and work in garter stitch (every row knit) for 20 rows.
Break yarn and draw through stitches.
Fasten off.

FACE
Use fawn.
Cast on 8 sts and work in stocking stitch.
K 1 row.
Next row: K1, P to last st, k1.
Next row: Increase 1 st at each

end of this and every following row until there are 20 sts, then on following 4th row to make 22 sts.

Work 9 rows without further shaping.

Decrease 1 st at each end of next and 2 following alt rows (16 sts).

Work 1 row.

Next row: K8, turn work, k1, P to the last st, k1.

Working on these stitches only, decrease 1 st at each end of next and every following alt row (4 sts).

K1, P to last st, k1.

Next row: K.

Next row: P.

K2tog twice (2 sts).

Break yarn and draw through. Fasten off.

Rejoin yarn to remaining 8 sts and complete to match first side.

EARS

Use brown.

Using yarn single, cast on 10 sts and work in garter stitch.

K 4 rows.

Next row: K2tog, k6, k2tog (8 sts).

Work 3 rows without shaping.

Next row: K2tog, k4, k2tog (6 sts).

Next row: K2tog, k2, k2tog (4 sts).

Next row: K2tog twice (2 sts).

Break yarn and draw through. Fasten off.

Make another ear to match.

VEST

Use green.

Cast on 30 sts.

Work in garter stitch.

K 1 row.

Next row: Increase 1 st at each end of row (32 sts).

Work 8 rows without shaping.

Shape armholes:

K7, bind off 2 sts, k10, bind off 2 sts, working on these 7 sts only.

K 9 rows.

Next row: Bind off 1 st, work to end.

K 1 row.

Next row: Bind off 1 st, work to end.

Work 3 rows.

Bind off.

Rejoin yarn to central 10 sts.

Work 14 rows in garter stitch.

Bind off.

Rejoin yarn to remaining 7 sts, reverse shaping to match first side.

SCARF

Use red.

Using yarn doubled, cast on 6 sts.

Work in garter stitch until scarf measures approx 10 in.

Bind off.

TO MAKE UP MONKEY

Darn in all loose ends. Join center seams of body fronts and attach to back with mattress stitch. Stuff firmly. Sew head pieces together and attach face. Sew arm and leg seams using mattress stitch and attach hands and feet. Using illustration as a guide, attach all body pieces. Sew on tail. Sew shoulders together on vest and tie scarf loosely around neck. Embroider facial features.

Robbie the fish

Robbie's brightly colored scales make him one of the best-looking fish in the sea. He is just the right size to tuck under your arm on a day out exploring dry land!

MATERIALS

- **Worsted yarn:**
  4 oz. white
  2 oz. light blue
  2 oz. mid-blue
  2 oz. lilac
- **Fingering yarn:**
  2 oz. gold (used doubled)
- Black embroidery thread for eyes
- Needles: size 6
- Toy stuffing

MAIN BODY

Use white.
Cast on 8 sts and K 1 row.
Beginning with a purl row, work in stocking stitch throughout.
Cast on 3 sts at the beginning of next 2 rows (14 sts).
Cast on 2 sts at the beginning of the next 4 rows (22 sts).
Work 1 row.
Next row: Increase 1 st at each end of this, and every following alt row, until there are 26 sts.

Next row: P.
Next row: Increase 1 st at each end of this and following 4 alternate rows, until there are 30 sts.
Work a further 7 rows without shaping.
Next row: Decrease 1 st at each end of this and following 4th row (26 sts).
Work 1 row.
Next row: Decrease 1 st at each end of this and every following alternate row, until there are 22 sts.
Work 1 row.
Bind off 2 sts at the beginning of the next 4 rows (14 sts).
Bind off 3 sts at the beginning of the next 2 rows (8 sts).
Bind off remaining 8 sts.
Make another piece to match.

SCALES

24 scales are used on the fish (12 on each side), and they are knitted in light blue, mid-blue, and lilac.

Using the appropriate yarn, cast on 3 sts and K 2 rows.
Next row: Increase 1 st at each end of row (5 sts).
Next row: P.
Repeat the last 2 rows until there are 13 sts.
Bind off.

FIN AND TAIL

The pieces are worked in exactly the same manner as the scales. Use gold.
Using yarn doubled, cast on 8 sts and, working in k1 p1 rib, complete 1 row.
Next row: Increase 1 st at each end of this row (10 sts).
Continue increasing as before, on every row, until there are 20 sts.
Bind off.

TO MAKE UP THE FISH

Darn in all loose ends. Attach 12 of the fins to each side panel as illustrated. When joining the side panels, insert the fin along the top edge and the tail at the back. Stuff firmly. Use black embroidery thread for the eyes, and sew on lips made from a scrap of gold yarn.

Mr. Bumble

Mr. Bumble is a jolly little bee. He is simple to knit and enjoys buzzing around the garden.

MATERIALS
- **Worsted yarn:**
  2 oz. black
- **Fingering yarn:**
  2 oz. gold*
- White and pink embroidery thread for eyes and mouth
- Needles: size 6
- Toy stuffing

* Yarn to be used doubled

BODY

TOP PANEL

Worked in black and gold, in stocking stitch 4 x 4 row stripes.
Using black, cast on 6 sts and work 2 rows in stocking stitch.
Increase in every stitch (12 sts).
Next row: P.
Increase in every stitch (24 sts).
Beginning with a purl row, work 29 rows in stocking stitch.
Decrease top.
Next row: K1, k2 tog, k8, k2tog, k8, k2tog, k1 (21 sts).

Beginning with a purl row, work 7 rows in stocking stitch.
Next row: K1, sl1, k1, psso, k15, k2tog, k1 (19 sts).
Next row: P.
Next row: K1, sl1, k1, psso, k13, k2tog, k1 (17 sts).
Next row: P.
Next row: K1, sl1, k1, psso, k11, k2tog, k1 (15 sts).
Next row: P.
Next row: K1, sl1, k1, psso, k9, k2tog, k1 (13 sts).
Next row: P.
Next row: Bind off 2 sts at the beginning of the next 4 rows (5 sts).
Bind off remainder.

BOTTOM PANEL
Work as for top panel, using black yarn only.

HEAD
Use black.
Cast on 6 sts.
Stocking stitch 2 rows.
Next row: Increase 1 st at each end of row (8 sts).
Stocking stitch 10 rows.
Next row: Decrease 1 st at each end of this row (6 sts).
Bind off.
Make another piece the same.

LARGE WINGS
Use black.
Cast on 12 sts.
K 2 rows.
Row 3: Increase 1 st at each end of the row (14 sts).
Repeat these 3 rows until there are 22 sts.
Next row: K2tog to end (11 sts).
Bind off.
Make another wing.

SMALL WINGS
Use black.
Cast on 8 sts.
K 2 rows.
Row 3: Increase 1 st at each end of row (10 sts).
Repeat these 3 rows until there are 18 sts.
Next row: K2tog to end (9 sts).
Bind off.
Make another wing.

TO MAKE UP THE BEE
Darn in all ends. Sew body pieces together with mattress stitch; stuff. Join head sections; attach to body. Use chain stitch to make antennae and knot the ends to form balls. Attach to head. Join wings to body. Embroider eyes and mouth.

Teddy bear

Create this enduring Teddy Bear to be someone's special friend. He will reward his owner with lots of love and loyalty. There are two different sweaters to make for him, so you can change his outfits and keep him looking stylish. He would also make a special gift for an adult bear fan.

MATERIALS

- **Worsted yarn:**
  8 oz. brown fleck
- Black embroidery thread for eyes and mouth
- Needles: size 6
- Toy stuffing

HEAD

Cast on 6 sts.
Work in garter stitch throughout.
Work 1 row.
Next row: Increase in every stitch (12 sts).
Work 1 row.
Next row: K1, increase into each of the next 10 sts, k1 (22 sts).
Work 1 row.

SHAPE NOSE

Next row: K1, inc 1, k7, inc 1, k6, inc 1, k7, inc 1, k1 (26 sts).
Next and every alt row: Work without shaping.
Next row: K1, inc 1, k9, inc 1, k6, inc 1, k9, inc 1, k1 (30 sts).
Next row: K1, inc 1, k11, inc 1, k6, inc 1, k11, inc 1, k1 (34 sts).
Next row: K1, inc 1, k13, inc 1, k6, inc 1, k13, inc 1, k1 (38 sts).
Next row: K1, inc 1, k15, inc 1, k6, inc 1, k15, inc 1, k1 (42 sts).
Work 2 rows without shaping.
Next row: (K1, k2tog) six times, k6, (k2tog, k1) six times (30 sts).

SHAPE HEAD

Next row: K11, inc 1, k1, inc 1, k6, inc 1, k1, inc 1, k11 (34 sts).
Next and every alt row: Work without shaping.
Next row: K12, inc 1, k1, inc 1, k8, inc 1, k1, inc 1, k12 (38 sts).
Next row: K13, inc 1, k1, inc 1, k10, inc 1, k1, inc 1, k13 (42 sts).
Next row: K14, inc 1, k1, inc 1, k12, inc 1, k1, inc 1, k14 (46 sts).
Next row: K15, inc 1, k1, inc 1, k14, inc 1, k1, inc 1, k15 (50 sts).
Next row: K16, inc 1, k1, inc 1, k16, inc 1, k1, inc 1, k16 (54 sts).
Next row: K6 (inc 1, k1) thirteen times, k16, (k1, inc 1) thirteen times, k6 (80 sts).
Work a further 13 rows without shaping.

SHAPE BACK

Next row: (K8, k2tog) to end (72 sts).
Next and every alt row: Work without shaping.
Next row: (K7, k2tog) to end (64 sts).
Next row: (K6, k2tog) to end (56 sts).
Next row (K5, k2tog) to end (48 sts).
Next row: (K4, k2tog) to end (40 sts).
Next row: (K3, k2tog) to end (32 sts).
Next row: (K2, k2tog) to end (24 sts).
Next row: (K1, k2tog) to end

(16 sts).
Next row: (K2tog) to end
(8 sts).
Bind off.

BODY
Cast on 9 sts.
Work 2 rows in garter stitch.
Next row: Increase 1 st at each
end of row (11 sts).
Work 1 row.
Repeat the last 2 rows, four
times (19 sts).
Next row: K9, increase before
and after center stitch, k9
(21 sts).
Continue to increase in this
manner (either side of center
stitch) on every alt row until
there are 45 sts.
Work a further 31 rows
without shaping.
Next row: Decrease 1 st at each
end of this and every following
alt row until there are 21 sts.
Next row: (K2tog) five times,
k1, (k2tog) five times.
Bind off.
Make another piece to match.

ARMS
Cast on 7 sts.
Work 1 row.

Next row: K1 (inc 1, k1) to end
(13 sts).
Repeat the last 2 rows once
more (25 sts).
Work 1 row.
Next row: K6, inc 1, k1, inc 1,
k11, inc 1, k1, inc 1, k6 (29 sts).
Work a further 28 rows
without shaping.

SHAPE TOP OF ARMS
Decrease 1 st at each end of
this and every following 6th
row until there are 17 sts, then
on every following 3rd row
until there are 11 sts.
Next row: K1 (k2tog) to end
(6 sts).
Bind off.
Make another piece to match.

LEGS
Cast on 46 sts.
Work 12 rows.
Next row: Decrease 1 st at each
end of row (44 sts).
Bind off 2 sts at the beg of the
next 2 rows (40 sts).
Bind off 4 sts at the beg of the
next 2 rows (32 sts).
Work a further 31 rows
without shaping.
Bind off 4 sts at the beg of the

next 2 rows (24 sts).
Bind off 4 sts at the beg of the
next 2 rows (16 sts).
Bind off remaining stitches.
Make another leg to match.

PAW PADS
Cast on 5 sts. Work in garter
stitch.
Work 1 row.
Next row: Increase 1 st, at each
end of this and every following
alt row, until there are 13 sts.
Work a further 6 rows without
shaping.
Next row: Decrease 1 st, at
each end of every alt row, until
there are 8 sts.
Bind off.
Make another pad to match.

EARS—2 PIECES EACH EAR
Beginning at the top of the
ear, cast on 16 sts.
Work in garter stitch.
Work 1 row.
Next row: Increase 1 st at each
end of the row (18 sts).
Work 1 row.
Repeat the last 2 rows until
there are 24 sts.
Work a further 2 rows without
shaping.

Next row: Decrease 1 st at each end of this and every following alt row, until there are 16 sts. Bind off.
Make four pieces in total.

TO MAKE UP THE BEAR

Darn in all loose ends. Join head seam and stuff firmly. Sew ear sections together and position on head as illustrated. Leaving neck open, join all body pieces and attach head. Join both leg seams, inserting pads at the base, and stuff firmly. Repeat with arms. Attach arms and legs to body, ensuring that Teddy will sit steadily! Embroider on the eyes and nose.

Pink sweater

MATERIALS

- **Worsted yarn:**
  4 oz. pink (A)
- **Fingering yarn:**
  2 oz. white (B) *
- Needles: size 6
- 2 small buttons

* Yarn to be used doubled

BACK

Using main yarn, cast on 50 sts.
Work 8 rows in k2 p2 rib.
Continue in stocking stitch, and work 40 rows.
Shoulder shaping:
Bind off 15 sts at the beginning of the next 2 rows (20 sts).
Bind off remaining sts.

FRONT

Using main yarn, cast on 50 sts.
Work 8 rows in k2 p2 rib.
Continue in stocking stitch, and work 4 rows.
Using Fair Isle technique and contrast yarn where indicated, work the next 11 rows from the chart.
Continue in stocking stitch until 34 rows have been completed from top of rib.

■ A
☐ B

Divide for neck.
K20, bind off central 10 sts, K to end.
Using these 20 sts only, work 1 row.
Next row: Decrease 1 st at neck edge on this and following two alt rows (17 sts).
Work 3 rows in stocking stitch.
Bind off.
Rejoin yarn to remaining 20 sts and work to match first side, reversing shapings.

SLEEVES

Using main yarn, cast on 40 sts.
Work 6 rows in k2 p2 rib.
Continue in stocking stitch, and work 20 rows.
Bind off.
Make another sleeve.

NECKBAND

Join right-hand shoulder using mattress stitch. With right side facing, pick up 54 sts evenly around the neck.
Work 5 rows in k2 p2 rib.
Bind off in pattern.

SHOULDER

Catch left side shoulder together at sleeve edge (approx 1 in.).
Pick up 32 sts evenly from neck edge, down to sleeve edge and back up to other side of neckband, and knit.
Next row: P.
Next row (buttonhole row):
K23, yfwd k2tog, k3, yfwd k2tog, k2.
Next row: P.
Bind off.

TO MAKE UP SWEATER

Darn in all ends and sew buttons to shoulder. Fold

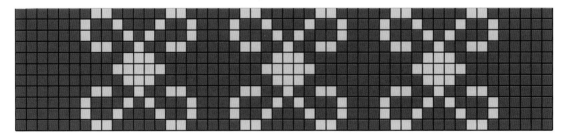

sleeves in half lengthwise and, starting at the center of the shoulder, sew on using mattress stitch. Join side and sleeve seams.

Blue sweater

MATERIALS
- **Worsted yarn:**
  4 oz. light blue
- Needles: size 6
- Cable needle

BACK
Cast on 50 sts.
Work 8 rows in k2 p2 rib.
Continue in stocking stitch and work 42 rows.
Work 6 rows in k2 p2 rib.
Bind off.

FRONT
Cast on 50 sts.
Work 8 rows in k2 p2 rib.
Continue in stocking stitch and work 42 rows, inserting cable panel in center of front panel —work 19 sts; set panel 13 sts; work 18 sts (50 sts).
Work 6 rows in k2 p2 rib.
Bind off.

SLEEVES
Work as for pink sweater.

TO MAKE UP SWEATER
Darn in all loose ends. Join front and back panels by a 1 in. seam at shoulders, using mattress stitch to form slash neck. Attach sleeves.

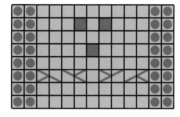

 Knit on RS, purl on WS

Purl on RS, knit on WS

Make bobble (k1, p1, k1, p1, k1) in stitch to make 5 sts from one.
Turn, p5, turn, and pass 2nd, 3rd, 4th, 5th sts over first st one at a time, then knit into the back of it.

Sl next 2 sts onto cable needle and hold at front.

K2, then p2 from cable needle.

Sl next 2 sts onto cable needle and hold at back.
P2, then k2 from cable needle.

Ricky rabbit

This delightful, floppy-eared bunny likes to dress to impress his friends in the warren, loves meeting new people, and has got a great sense of humor. Who are you going to introduce him to?

MATERIALS

- **Worsted yarn:**
  4 oz. fawn
  4 oz. cream
- Black embroidery thread for eyes and mouth
- ½ yd. broad double satin ribbon
- Needles: size 5
- Toy stuffing

BODY—FRONT

Use cream. Cast on 20 sts and work 2 rows in stocking stitch. Increase 1 st at each end of next and following alternate row (24 sts).
Continue without further shaping until work measures 6 in. from beginning.
Next row: Decrease 1 st at each end of next and every following 4th row until there are 12 sts.
Work 3 rows in stocking stitch. Bind off.

BODY—BACK

Use fawn.
Cast on 24 sts and work 2 rows in stocking stitch.
Increase 1 st at each end of this and following alternate row (28 sts).
Continue without further shaping until work measures 6 in. from beginning.
Next row: Decrease 1 st at each end of next and every following 4th row until there are 16 sts.
Work 3 rows in stocking stitch. Bind off.

HEAD—BACK

Use fawn. Cast on 12 sts and work 2 rows in stocking stitch.
Next row: Increase 1 st at each end of row (14 sts).
Repeat this increase on every other row until there are 20 sts.
Work a further 8 rows in stocking stitch without shaping.
Next row: Decrease 1 st at each end of this and every following alternate row until there are 6 sts.
Bind off.

HEAD—FRONT

Use fawn.
Cast on 6 sts and work 2 rows in stocking stitch.
Next row: K1, increase 1 st, K to end of row (7 sts).
Next row: K1, P to last stitch, increase 1 st, k1 (8 sts).
Repeat the last 2 rows four times (16 sts).
Work a further 2 rows without shaping.
Next row: K2tog, K to end (15 sts).
Next row: P.
Repeat the last 2 rows four times (9 sts).
Continue to decrease on the same edge until 3 sts remain.
Next row: K1, p2tog. Bind off.
Work another piece the same, reversing all shaping.

EARS

Each made in two sections (one in fawn and one in cream).

following 4th row, until there are 11 sts.
Work a further 11 rows without shaping.
Next row: Decrease at each end of this and every following 8th row until 3 sts remain.
Next row: K1, p2tog, psso. Fasten off.

FEET
Use fawn.
Cast on 8 sts and work 2 rows in stocking stitch.
Next row: Increase 1 st at each end of row (10 sts).
Continue working in stocking stitch for a further 31 rows without shaping.
Bind off.
Make another foot to match.

ARMS
Use fawn.
Follow arm pattern for Mousie Mousie (see pages 70–71).
Make another arm to match.

TAIL
Use cream.
Make a pompom. Cut 2 circles of cardboard, approx 8 in. in diameter, and cut out a circle in the center of each to make a ring. Hold both rings together and start wrapping yarn around the ring, threading it through the center, until completely covered. Position the point of a pair of scissors in the yarn loops so that you can cut through them, going in between the cardboard rings. Separate the rings slightly and tie yarn tightly inside the cut sections. Remove cardboard and fluff up the pompom. Sew to back of rabbit.

TO MAKE UP THE RABBIT
Join body pieces together using mattress stitch; stuff. Join side seams of both feet and arms, and pad slightly. Attach arms to shoulders of rabbit and sew on feet as illustrated. To form head, sew the shaped sides of the two front pieces together, then sew straight edge to back piece, leaving the cast-on edges open to stuff. Attach to body. Sew a cream and a fawn ear piece together. Repeat to make the other ear and attach to head. Embroider features. Tie ribbon around neck.

Using the appropriate yarn, cast on 5 sts and knit one row.
Next row: K1, P to last st, k1.
Continue working in stocking stitch, increasing 1 st at each end of next and every

Sleeveless top

MATERIALS

- **Worsted yarn:**
  2 oz. light blue
- Needles: size 7

BACK

Cast on 22 sts.

Knit 2 rows.

Next row: Continue in stocking stitch until work measures 3 in., ending with a WS row *.

SHAPE TOP OF BACK

K1, k2tog, work to last 3 sts, k2tog, k1 (20 sts).

Work 3 rows in stocking stitch.

Repeat the last 4 rows once more (18 sts).

Then work the decrease row once more (16 sts).

Next row: P.

Bind off.

FRONT

Work as for Back until you reach *.

Shape top and divide for neck: k1, k2tog, k5, k2tog, k1.

Turn work and work on these 9 sts only.

Stocking stitch 3 rows.

Next row: K1, k2tog, k3, k2tog, k1 (7 sts).

Stocking stitch 3 rows.

Next row: K1, k2tog, k1, k2tog, k1 (5 sts).

Stocking stitch 3 rows.

Bind off.

Rejoin yarn to remaining sts, complete to match first side and bind off.

TO MAKE UP RABBIT'S TOP

Darn in all ends. Join shoulder seams using mattress stitch. Join side seams.

Penguin

Penguin is just the right size for little hands. She's ready to waddle into a new home and become a cherished companion. She has lots of stories to tell about her life in the Arctic, exploring snowy wastes and diving through the ice.

MATERIALS

- **Worsted yarn:**
  2 oz. black
  2 oz. white
- **Fingering yarn:**
  2 oz. gold *
- Black embroidery thread
- Needles: size 6
- Toy stuffing

*Yarn to be used doubled

BACK
Use black.
Cast on 20 sts and, working in stocking stitch, complete 26 rows.
Decrease 1 st at each end of next and every following 6th row until there are 10 sts.
Work 1 row *.
Decrease 1 st at each end of next and every following alt row until there are 6 sts.
Work 1 row.
Next row: K2tog, k2, k2tog (4 sts).
Next row: P.
Bind off.

FRONT
Use white.
Work as back until *.
Bind off.

BEAK TOP
Use gold.
Using yarn doubled, cast on 18 sts.
Work 4 rows in stocking stitch.
Decrease 1 st at each end of next 4 rows (10 sts).
Work 12 rows without further shaping.
Decrease 1 st at each end of next 3 rows (4 sts).
Next row: P.
Bind off.

BEAK BOTTOM
Use gold.
Using yarn doubled, cast on 5 sts.
Work 4 rows in stocking stitch.
Next row: K2tog, k1, k2tog (3 sts).
Starting with a purl row, work 13 rows in stocking stitch.
Next row: K1, k2tog (2 sts).

Purl.
Break yarn off, draw through loops, and fasten off.

FEET
(Make two in black and two in gold.)
Using the appropriate yarn, cast on 7 sts.
Work 2 rows in stocking stitch.
Increase 1 st at each end of this and every following alternate row until there are 11 sts.
Work 5 rows in stocking stitch.
Decrease 1 st at each end of next and every following alternate row until there are 5 sts.
Purl.
Bind off.

LEFT FLIPPER
Use black.
Cast on 3 sts.
Work 1 row in purl.
Next row: * Increase 1 st at beginning of this and every following alternate row until

there are 10 sts.
Work 16 rows in stocking
stitch.
Shape top of flipper:
Work to last 3 sts, k2tog, k1
(9 sts).
Next row: P.

Continue to decrease at the
end of next and every
following alternate row until
there are 5 sts.
Work 1 row.
Bind off.

RIGHT FLIPPER
Work as Left Flipper to *.
Increase 1 st at end of this and
every following alternate row
until there are 10 sts.
Work 16 rows in stocking
stitch.
Complete to match left side,
reversing shaping at the top.

TO MAKE UP PENGUIN
Darn in all loose ends. Join
main body panels using
mattress stitch, leaving the top
open. Stuff firmly. Join beak
parts, stuffing them slightly.
Attach beak to top of body as
illustrated, and stitch the eyes
in black embroidery thread.
Using mattress stitch, join the
black and gold feet pieces,
padding them firmly. Close
them completely and then
attach to the main body, with
the gold showing on top.
Apply flippers to each side of
the main body along
side seam.

Kangaroo and baby roo

This cute and cuddly double act have traveled a long way from sunny Australia. Kangaroo has prepared for chilly breezes with a dashing scarf; Baby Roo just snuggles down in the pouch. They're just looking for someone to show them all the sights in their new home country.

MATERIALS

- **Worsted yarn:**
  8 oz. gold
  2 oz. cream
  2 oz. green
- Black embroidery thread for eyes
- Needles: size 6, size 5, size 2–3
- Toy stuffing

Use size 6 needles for the kangaroo.

BODY—SIDE
Use gold.
Cast on 34 sts.
Work 9 rows in stocking stitch.
Next row: Bind off 16 sts, P to end (18 sts).
Row 11: K to last st, inc at end of row (19 sts).
Row 12: Inc 1 st at beg of row, P to end (20 sts).
Row 13: K to last st, inc at end of row (21 sts).
Row 14: As row 12 (22 sts).

Row 15: K.
Row 16: As row 12 (23 sts).
Row 17: K.
Row 18: P (24 sts).
Work a further 15 rows in stocking stitch without shaping.
Row 34: P2tog, work to end (23 sts).
Row 35: K.
Row 36: Bind off 7 sts, P to end (16 sts).
Row 37: K to last st, inc at end of row (17 sts).
Row 38: P.
Row 39: As row 37 (18 sts).
Work a further 3 rows in stocking stitch without shaping.
Row 43: K2tog, K to end (17 sts).
Row 44: P.
Row 45: As row 43 (16 sts).
Row 46: P.
Row 47: As row 43 (15 sts).
Row 48: P.
Row 49: As row 43 (14 sts).

Work a further 8 rows in stocking stitch without shaping.
Row 58: Dec 1 st at beg of row, work to end (13 sts).
Row 59: Dec 1 st at beg of row, work to end (12 sts).
Work a further 6 rows in stocking stitch without shaping.
Row 66: Cast on 7 sts, work to end (19 sts).
Row 67: K.
Row 68: P2tog, work to end (18 sts).
Row 69: K.
Row 70: As row 68 (17 sts).
Row 71: K.
Row 72: As row 68 (16 sts).
Row 73: K2tog, work to end.
Row 74: As row 68 (15 sts).
Row 75: K2tog, work to end (14 sts).
Row 76: K2tog, work to last 2 sts, k2tog (12 sts).
Row 77: K2tog at each end of row (10 sts).

Bind off.
Make another piece, reversing all shaping.

BODY—FRONT
Use cream.
Cast on 40 sts.
Work 9 rows in stocking stitch.
Row 10: Bind off 16 sts, work to end (24 sts).
Row 11: Bind off 16 sts, work to end (8 sts).
Row 12: Increase 1 st at each end of row (10 sts).
Row 13: Increase 1 st at each end of row (12 sts).
Row 14: Increase 1 st at each end of row (14 sts).
Row 15: K.
Row 16: Increase 1 st at each end of row (16 sts).
Row 17: K.
Row 18: Increase 1 st at each end of row (18 sts).
Row 19: K.
Row 20: Increase 1 st at each end of row (20 sts).
Work a further 17 rows without shaping.
Row 38: Bind off 6 sts at beg of row, work to end (14 sts).
Row 39: Bind off 6 sts at beg of row, work to end (8 sts).

Work on these 8 sts until work measures the same as the body sides to beg of head shaping. Bind off.

BODY—BASE
Use gold.
Cast on 10 sts.
Work 18 rows in stocking stitch.
Bind off.

EARS
Use gold.
Cast on 7 sts.
Work 8 rows in garter stitch (every row knit).
Next row: K2tog, k3, k2tog (5 sts).
Next row: K.
Next row: K2tog, k1, k2tog (3 sts).
Next row: K.
Next row: K2tog, k1 (2 sts).
Next row: K2tog (1 st).
Fasten off.
Make another ear to match.

ARMS
Use gold.
Follow arm instructions for Mousie Mousie (see pages 70–71).

Make two arms.

TAIL
Use gold.
Follow tail instructions for Mousie Mousie (see pages 70–71) and work 28 rows without shaping.

POUCH
Using size 6 needles, cast on 14 sts.
Moss stitch 1 row.
Next row: Continue in moss stitch and Increase 1 st at each end of row (16 sts).
Work 2 rows without shaping.
Continue to increase 1 st at each end of next and every following 3rd row until there are 22 sts.
Next row: Work in k1 p1 rib to end.
Work 2 rows in rib without further shaping.
Bind off in pattern.

SCARF
Use green.
Using size 2–3 needles, cast on 7 sts and garter stitch (every row knit) for approx 8 in.
Bind off.

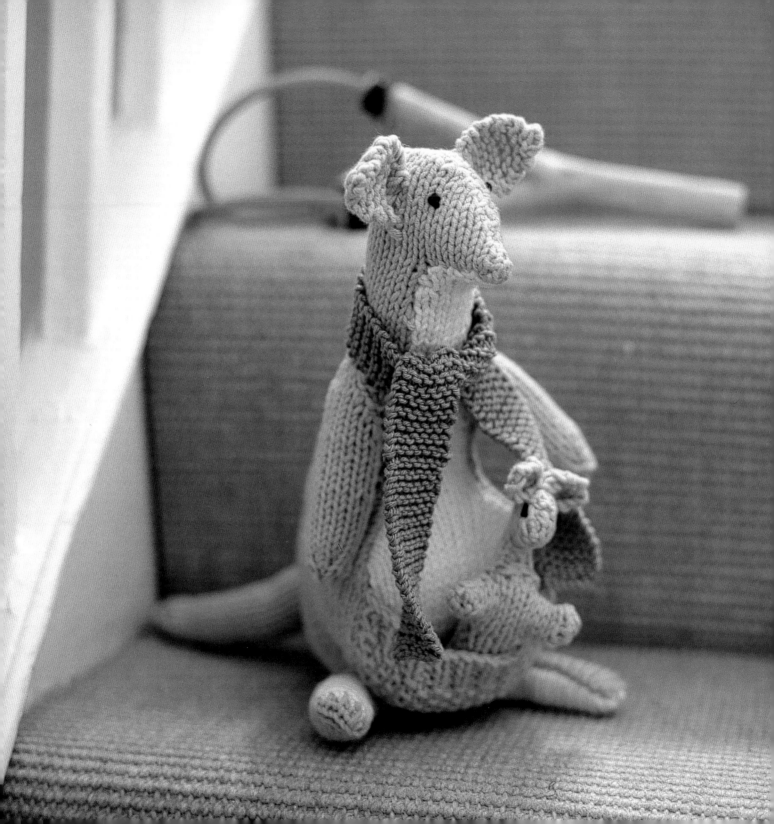

TO MAKE UP KANGAROO

Darn in all loose ends. Sew two body sides together using mattress stitch, and attach to front panel. Stuff firmly, ensuring the base is squarely placed at the bottom. Attach pouch to body using mattress stitch. Join arm and tail seams and stuff. Sew arms to main body at shoulder, and position tail at base. Embroider eyes. Tie scarf loosely around neck.

BABY ROO

Use gold and size 5 needles.

BODY—SIDE PANEL

Starting at feet, cast on 10 sts.
Work 4 rows in stocking stitch.
5th row: Bind off 5 sts, K to end (5 sts).
Work a further 7 rows without shaping.
13th row: Cast on 4 sts, K to end (9 sts).
Work a further 3 rows without shaping.
17th row: Bind off 4 sts, K to end (5 sts).
Work a futher 2 rows without shaping.
20th row: P2tog, p3 (4 sts).

21st row: K.
22nd row: P2tog, p2 (3 sts).
23rd row: Cast on 4 sts, K to end (7 sts).
24th row: P2tog, P to end (6 sts).
25th row: K2tog, K to end (5 sts).
26th row: P.
27th row: K2tog, k3.
Bind off.
Work second side to match this, reversing all shaping.

BODY—FRONT PANEL

Cast on 14 sts.
Work 4 rows in stocking stitch.
5th row: Bind off 5 sts, K to end (9 sts).
6th row: Bind off 5 sts, P to end (4 sts).
Work a further 8 rows without shaping.
15th row: Cast on 4 sts, K to end (8 sts).
16th row: Cast on 4 sts, P to end (12 sts).
Work a further 3 rows without shaping.
20th row: Bind off 4 sts, P to end (8 sts).
21st row: Bind off 4 sts, K to end (4 sts).

22nd row: P2tog twice.
23rd row: K2tog, fasten off.

EARS

Cast on 2 sts.
Work 4 rows in garter stitch.
Next row: K2tog twice.
Next row: K2.
Next row: K2tog, fasten off.
Make another ear to match.

TAIL

Cast on 4 sts.
Work 16 rows in garter stitch.
Next row: K2tog twice.
Next row: K2.
Next row: K2tog, fasten off.

TO MAKE UP BABY ROO

Darn in all loose ends. Sew the two sides together along back seam and leave a small opening for stuffing. Sew in front panel, starting at bottom feet. Stuff firmly and close seam in the back. Sew in ears, folding them slightly at the base. Attach tail. Embroider the eyes.

Loulou the elephant

Share all your secrets with Loulou, a gentle wooly giant, who will never forget them.
This sturdy creature is a delight to knit.

MATERIALS

- **Worsted yarn:**
  8 oz. gray
- **Fingering yarn:**
  Remnants of white
- Needles: size 6, size 2–3
- Toy stuffing

Use size 6 needles and gray yarn for all parts of elephant except for tusks.

HEAD—SIDE SECTIONS

Cast on 25 sts.
Knit 1 row.
Continue in stocking stitch throughout. Increase 1 st at each end of the next 2 rows (29 sts).
Work a further 11 rows without shaping.
Next row: Increase 1 st at each end of row (31 sts).
Work a further 12 rows without shaping.
Next row: K2tog at each end of row (29 sts).
Work a further 14 rows without shaping.
Next row: K2tog at each end of the following 5 rows (19 sts).
Bind off.
Make another piece to match.

HEAD—CENTER GUSSET, TOP

Cast on 9 sts.
Work 7 rows in stocking stitch.
Next row: Increase 1 st at each end of row (9 sts).
Repeat the last 8 rows seven times (23 sts).
Work a further 30 rows without shaping.
Next row: Decrease 1 st at each end of row (21 sts).
Work a further 11 rows without shaping.
Repeat the last 1 row eight times (5 sts).
Bind off.

HEAD—CENTER GUSSET, UNDER TRUNK

Cast on 7 sts.
Work 11 rows in stocking stitch.
Next row: Increase 1 st at each end of row.
Repeat the last 12 rows five times.
Bind off.

EARS

Ears are worked in garter stitch throughout.
Cast on 17 sts.
Knit 1 row.
Next row: Increase 1 st at each end of the following 6 rows (29 sts).
Next row: K to last stitch, increase twice (31 sts).
Work a further 18 rows without shaping.
Next row: (K2tog, k3) to last st, k1 (25 sts).
Next row: K2tog three times, k5, k2tog three times.
Bind off remaining stitches.
Make another ear to match.

BODY—FRONT AND BACK

Cast on 20 sts.
Work in stocking stitch throughout.
Work 2 rows.
Next row: Increase 1 st at each end of this and every following alternate row until there are 30 sts.
Next row: Increase 1 st at each end of this and every following 4th row until there are 40 sts.

Work a further 24 rows without shaping.
Next row: Decrease 1 st at each end of this and every following 4th row until there are 20 sts.
Next row: K2tog, K to end.
Bind off.

ARMS
Cast on 25 sts.
Work 22 rows in stocking stitch.
Bind off.
Make another arm to match.

LEGS
Cast on 30 sts.
Work 30 rows in stocking stitch.
Bind off.
Make another leg to match.

PADS—FOR ARMS
Cast on 6 sts.
Work 2 rows in stocking stitch.
Next row: Increase 1 st at each end of row (8 sts).
Next row: P.
Next row: Increase 1 st at each end of row (10 sts).
Work a further 5 rows without shaping.
Next row: Decrease 1 st at each

end of following 2 alt rows (6 sts).
Bind off.
Make another pad to match.

PADS—FOR LEGS
Cast on 6 sts.
Work 2 rows in stocking stitch.
Next row: Increase 1 st at each end of this and following 2 alternate rows (12 sts).
Work a further 5 rows without shaping.
Next row: Decrease 1 st at each end of this and following 2 alt rows (6 sts).
Bind off.
Make another pad to match.

TAIL
Cast on 7 sts.
Work 14 rows in stocking stitch.
Next row: Decrease 1 st at each end of this and every following 4th row until there are 3 sts.
Work a further 3 rows without shaping.
Break yarn and draw through remaining stitches. Fasten off.
Cut short lengths of yarn, knot together, place in the point of

the tail, and sew side seam using mattress stitch.

TUSKS
Use size 2–3 needles and white yarn.
Cast on 7 sts.
Work in stocking stitch for 30 rows.
Next row: K1, k2tog, k1, k2tog, k1 (5 sts).
Next row: P.
Next row: K2tog, k1, k2tog (3 sts).
Next row: P.
Next row: K3tog and fasten off.
Make another tusk to match.

TO MAKE UP THE ELEPHANT
Darn in all loose ends. Join all pieces using mattress stitch. Attach sides of head to main gusset. Insert lower gusset and stuff, leaving neck edges open. Join body sections and sew on head. Sew side seams of arms and legs and insert pads; stuff. Attach to body (make sure elephant will sit on a flat surface). Sew on tail. Join tusk seams and draw up to make the tusk curve slightly. Sew on under the trunk. Add features.

Mousie Mousie

Childhood memories have been recaptured in this cute little mouse—my brothers kept mice and always had lots of fun with them! Mousie Mousie is a personable character who sports a wooly scarf to keep him snug. He's got a friendly face, a slithery tail, and would be good company for any child.

MATERIALS

- **Worsted yarn:**
  2 oz. fawn
  2 oz. cream
  2 oz. green
- Remnants of black embroidery thread for eyes
- Needles: size 6
- Double-pointed needles: 2 x size 6

HEAD

Use fawn.
Make two pieces. Please note that one piece must be knitted in reverse stocking stitch.
Cast on 17 sts.
Stocking stitch 2 rows.
Inc 1 st at each end of next and every following alt row until there are 27 sts.
Work 4 rows without shaping.
Next row: K1, (k2tog) twice, K to last 3 sts, k2tog, k1 (24 sts).
Next row: P.
Repeat the last two rows once more (21 sts).

Decrease 1 st at each end of next and every following alt row until there are 13 sts.
Next row: P.
Bind off 4 sts at the beginning of next 2 rows (5 sts).
Bind off remaining 5 sts.

EARS

Use fawn.
Cast on 7 sts. Knit in garter stitch.
Knit 2 rows.
Increase in first and last stitch of next row (9 sts).
Next row: K.
Increase in first and last stitch of next row (11 sts).
Next row: K.
Work 3 increase rows as before (17 sts).
Garter stitch 3 rows.
K2tog at each end of every row until there are 9 sts.
Garter stitch 1 row.
Bind off.
Make another ear to match.

BODY—FRONT

Use cream.
Cast on 5 sts. Knit in stocking stitch.
Increase either side of center stitch (7 sts).
Work 1 row.
Increase at the beginning and end of row, and as before on either side of center st (11 sts).
Work 1 row.
Repeat the last 2 rows until there are 39 sts.
Work 2 rows without shaping.
Decrease 1 st at each end of work on next and every alt row until there are 29 sts.
Decrease on either side of center stitch only, on next and every alt row until 17 sts remain.
Work 1 row.
Bind off.

BODY—BACK

Use fawn.
Cast on 5 sts.

1st row: Increase in every st.
2nd row: P.
3rd row: Increase 1 st at each end of next and every alt row until there are 22 sts.
Stocking stitch 4 rows.
Dec 1 st at each end of row (20 sts).
Work 1 row.
Repeat last 2 rows until there are 14 sts.
Continue without shaping until work matches front body section.
Bind off.

ARMS
Use fawn.
Cast on 6 sts.
Stocking stitch 2 rows.
Increase 1 st at each end of next and following alt rows until there are 14 sts.
Work 1 row.
Stocking stitch 16 rows.
K1 (k2tog) six times, k1 (8 sts).
Work 1 row without shaping.
K2tog to end (4 sts).
Break thread and draw through remaining sts and secure.
Make another arm to match.

FEET
Use fawn.
Cast on 8 sts.
Stocking stitch 2 rows.
Increase in first and last st of next row (10 sts).
Stocking stitch 18 rows.
Bind off.
Make another foot to match.

SCARF
Use light green.
Cast on 10 sts.
Garter stitch to length required: approx 12 in.
Bind off.

Use cream.
Using two double-pointed needles, cast on 7 sts.
Knit to end. Instead of turning work, slide from one end of the needle to the other, keeping right side facing at all times, and continue to knit.
This forms a tube.
Knit to desired length.
Bind off.

TO MAKE UP
MOUSIE MOUSIE
Join head pieces using mattress stitch and stuff. Join front and back body pieces in the same manner and secure to head. Sew on ears and tail. Join arm seams and stuff arms slightly; sew into position. Join seams of feet and sew pieces into a round. Sew to body, ensuring that they are in a position for the mouse to stand. Darn in the ends of the scarf and wrap around. Sew eyes and nose, using black embroidery thread as illustrated.

Reggie the snake

Have fun with this easy-to-knit snake. He will bring a smile to the face of any little boy.

MATERIALS
- **Worsted yarn:**
  4 oz. green
  2 oz. red *
- Remnants of yarn or embroidery thread for eyes and detail on back
- Needles: size 6
- Toy stuffing

*Yarn to be used doubled

MAIN BODY
Use green.
Cast on 7 sts and, working in stocking stitch, complete 2 rows.
Row 3: Increase 1 st at each end of work (9 sts).
Row 4: P.
Row 5: K.
Row 6: P.
Row 7: Increase 1 st at each end of work (11 sts).
Repeat the last 4 rows once

more until there are 13 sts.
Continue in stocking stitch for a further 13 rows without shaping.
Next row: Increase 1 st at each end of row (15 sts).
Work a further 13 rows without shaping.
Increase on next and every 14th row until there are 29 sts.
Work without further shaping until snake measures 41 in. from cast-on, ending on a purl row.

SHAPE HEAD
With RS facing, k14, bind off 1 st and K to end.
Working on the first 14 sts only, P.
Next row: K2tog, work to last 2 sts, k2tog (12 sts).
Work 3 rows without shaping.
Repeat the last 4 rows until 4 sts remain.
Bind off.
Rejoin yarn to remaining 14 sts and complete to match first side.

MOUTH LINING
Use red.
Using yarn doubled, cast on 4 sts and stocking stitch 2 rows.
Next row: Increase 1 st at each end of the row (6 sts).
Work 3 rows in stocking stitch.
Next row: Increase 1 st at each end of the row (8 sts).
Repeat the last 4 rows until there are 28 sts.
Work a further 12 rows without shaping.
With RS facing, decrease 1 st at each end of row.
Work 3 rows in stocking stitch.
Repeat the last 4 rows until 4 sts remain.
Bind off.

TO MAKE UP SNAKE
Darn in all loose ends. Join side seams using mattress stitch and stuff firmly. Insert mouth piece and slightly pad head.
Embroider eyes and detail on the back of the snake as illustrated.

Nursery toys
and accessories

Each of these projects is designed to entertain babies and young children. From the starfish to the finger puppets, they're all very easy to knit; give them individual character by experimenting with different colors and facial expressions. The nursery balls and blocks are classic toys, which would make perfect gifts for a baby shower. The two knitted bags will delight any little girl—she can use them to carry her treasures around or to store toys in.

Starfish

Living by the beach, I always hoped to find a beautiful starfish just like this one amongst the pebbles. Keep him to remind you of sunny days by the sea. He's ideal for a baby or young child to cuddle, and would even make a great doorstop!

MATERIALS
- Worsted yarn:
  2 oz. cream
  2 oz. light blue
  2 oz. sea blue
- Needles: size 7
- Toy stuffing

Knit ten panels: five are cream; five are a mixture of blues.

PANEL
Cast on 3 sts and stocking stitch 2 rows.
Next row: Increase 1 st at each end of next and every following 6th row until there are 19 sts.
Next row: P.

SHAPE TOP OF PANEL
K1, k2tog, K to last 3 sts, k2tog, k1 (17 sts).
Next row: P.
Repeat the last two rows until 5 sts remain.
K1, k2tog, pass stitch back from the right-hand needle to the left-hand needle, k2tog, k1 (3 sts).
Break yarn and draw through.

TO MAKE UP THE STARFISH
Darn in all ends.
Join all sections, leaving adequate seams to allow for stuffing. Close all seams using mattress stitch.

Nursery ball

These delightful knitted toys will be a welcome addition to any nursery. They are made in a combination of hearts and stripes.

MATERIALS
(Ball with hearts)
- **Fingering yarn:**
  2 oz. white (A)
  2 oz. sea green (B)

(Ball with stripes)
- **Fingering yarn:**
  2 oz. white
  2 oz. muted pink
  2 oz. sky blue
- Needles: size 2–3
- Toy stuffing

Each nursery ball uses approximately 2 oz. yarn.

Each ball is made up of 6 panels.

PANEL
Cast on 1 st, k1.
Next row: Purl into front, back and front (3 sts).
Continue in stocking stitch, increasing 1 st at each end of next and following 2 alternate rows (9 sts).
Work 2 rows without shaping.
Increase 1 st at each end of next and following 3rd row,

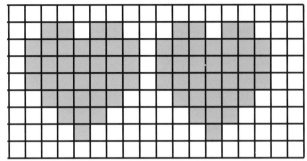

☐ **A**

▢ **B**

then at each end of following 4th row (15 sts).

Work 5 rows without further shaping.

Increase at each end of next and following 6th row. (19 sts). Work 9 rows without further shaping.

(Set heart motif within these 9 straight rows if required – follow chart.)

Decrease once at each end of next and every following 6th row until there are 13 sts.

Decrease at each end of following 4th row, following 3rd row and next alternate row (7 sts).

Work 1 row, then decrease 1 st at each end of the next 2 rows (3 sts).

Next row: Sl1, k2tog, psso. Fasten off.

For striped version, work as above, changing color every two rows.

TO MAKE UP THE BALL

Darn in all loose ends. Mattress stitch pieces together alternating the striped and plain, or motif and plain sections. Leave one seam open for inserting stuffing. Stuff, then close last seam.

Nursery blocks

Keep your toddlers happy with these pretty nursery blocks. They are knitted with motifs, interesting textures, and a variety of colors.

MATERIALS
(Block with hearts)
- **Fingering yarn:**
  2 oz. sky blue (A)
  2 oz. white (B)
  2 oz. lilac
  2 oz. muted green (C)

(Blocks with anchors)
- **Fingering yarn:**
  2 oz. white
  2 oz. light brown
  2 oz. sky blue

- Needles: size 2–3
- Toy stuffing
- Bell(s) (optional)

Each nursery block uses approximately 2 oz. yarn. Each block is made up of 6 squares.

PLAIN OR HEART SQUARE
Cast on 27 sts and moss stitch 3 rows.

Next row: Keeping a border of 3 moss sts on either side, stocking stitch 30 rows (insert heart motif in center if required—follow chart: work 4 sts, set motif 19 sts, work 4 sts).
Moss stitch 3 rows.
Bind off.

□ A   ■ B   □ C

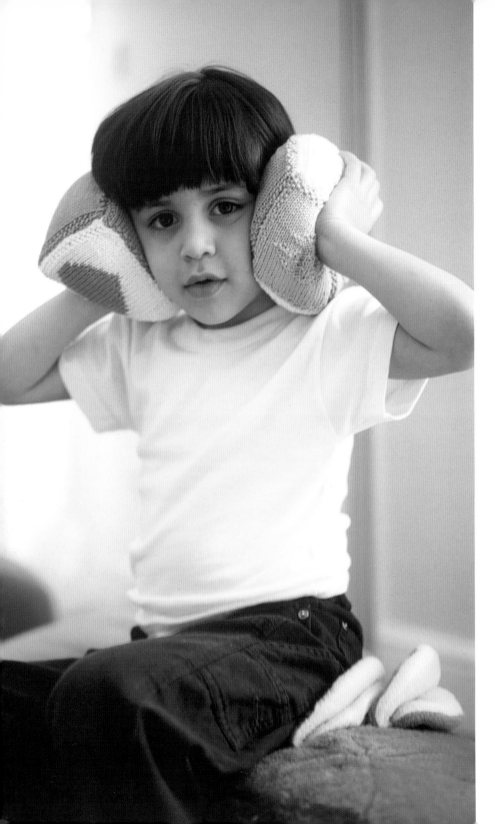

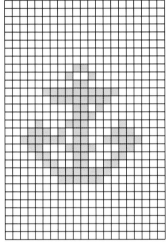

☐ **K on RS, P on WS**
☐ **P on RS, K on WS**

TO MAKE UP NURSERY
BLOCK
Darn in all ends. Join all
squares using mattress stitch,
leaving small opening for
stuffing.
Insert bell, if required, at this
stage. Stuff. Close seam.

Finger puppets

Children can create their own production with these finger puppets! They will ensure imaginative play and give hours of pleasure. Once you've mastered the simple pattern for the basic body, and have tried the octopus and mouse, delight and amuse your children by devising your own creatures to add to the cast.

MATERIALS
- **Fingering yarn:** remnants
- **Needles:** size 2–3
- **Toy stuffing**

BASIC BODY
Cast on 15 sts.
Knit 2 rows.
Continue in stocking stitch, beginning with a knit row, until work measures 2½ in. from cast-on; end on a purl row *.
Next row: Shape top. (K1, k2tog), repeat to end (10 sts).
Next row: P.
Next row: (K2tog) to end (5 sts).
Break yarn and draw through remaining stitches. Fasten off and join seam.

Octopus

BODY
Use blue yarn. Follow instructions for basic body to *.
Next row (make head): Increase. K1, * make 1, k1, repeat from * to end of row (29 sts).
Work 11 rows in moss stitch.
Next row: Decrease. K1, * k2tog, repeat from * to end (15 sts).
Next row: P.
Next row: K1, * k2tog, repeat from * to end (8 sts).
Break yarn and draw through remaining stitches. Fasten off.

LEGS
Using a contrasting shade of blue, cast on 5 sts.
Continue in stocking stitch until work measures 3 in.
Bind off.
Make a total of 8 legs.

TO MAKE UP THE OCTOPUS

Darn in all loose ends.
Join main seam on head and
body piece; stuff head section.
With running stitch, sew
around bottom of head and
draw up and secure (enclosing
stuffing). Attach legs evenly
around the body at the
bottom of the head.
Embroider smiley face as
illustrated.

Mouse

BODY

Using cream yarn, follow
instructions for basic body.

TAIL

Using cream yarn, cast on 5 sts.
Work in stocking stitch for
4½ in.
Next row: K2tog, k1, k2tog
(3 sts).
Next row: P.
Next row: K3tog.
Bind off.
Pull work slightly—this allows
it to coil into a roll.

EARS

Using cream yarn, cast on 4 sts.
Work 2 rows in stocking stitch.
Next row: Continue in stocking
stitch, increasing 1 st at each
end of this and every alt row,
until there are 14 sts.
Work a further 3 rows without
shaping.
Next row: Decrease 1 st at
each end of this and every
following row until there are
2 sts.
Next row: K2tog, fasten off.
Make another ear to match.

TO MAKE UP MOUSE

Darn in all loose ends. Attach
tail and ears. Embroider face
and whiskers as illustrated.

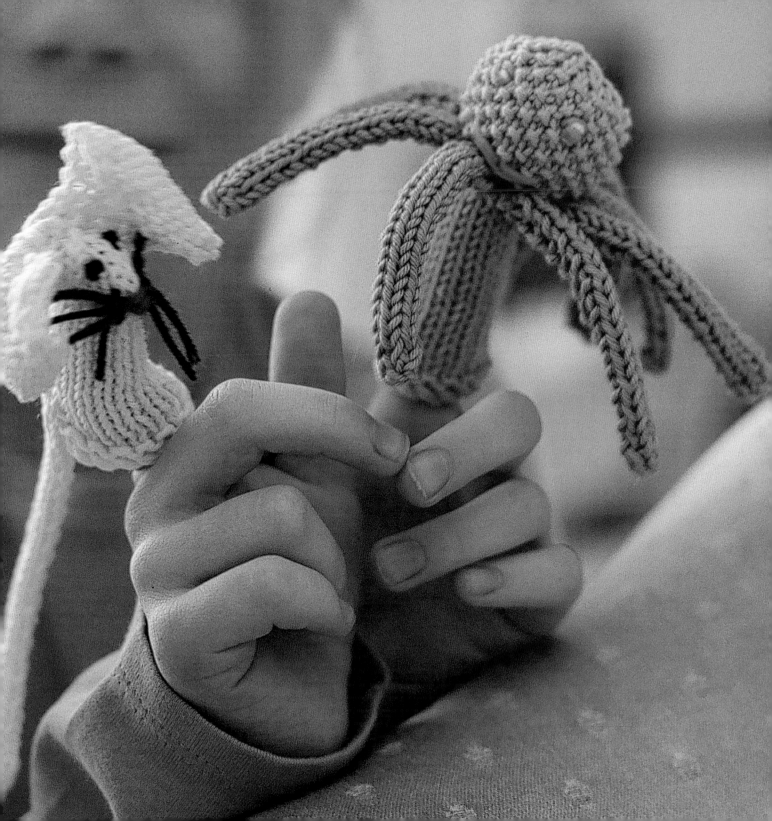

Cat nightdress case

Tuck your nightdress safely away and this smiley cat will keep it warm. She likes to laze around on the bed all day and be nearby for last-minute cuddles before bedtime.

MATERIALS

- **Worsted yarn:**
  4 oz. gold
- Black embroidery thread for eyes and mouth
- Needles: size 7
- Remnant of fabric:
  27½ in. x 23½ in.
- Lining (optional):
  27½ in. x 23½ in.
- Ribbon to decorate: 1 yd.
- Toy stuffing

HEAD—SIDES

Cast on 17 sts and work 6 rows in garter stitch (every row knit).

Next row: Increase 1 st at beg of row, K to end (18 sts).

Next row: K to last stitch, increase in last st (19 sts).

Next row: Cast on 7 sts, K to end (26 sts).

Work 5 rows without shaping.

Next row: K to last st, increase in last st (27 sts).

Work 7 rows without shaping.

Next row: K2tog, K to end (26 sts).

Next row: K to last 2 sts, k2tog (25 sts).

Repeat the last 2 rows six times (19 sts).

Work 1 row.

Next row: K to last 2 sts, k2tog (18 sts).

Next row: K2tog, K to last 2 sts, k2tog (16 sts).

Work 1 row.

Repeat the last 2 rows twice (12 sts).

Bind off.

Work another piece to match.

HEAD—GUSSET

Starting at nose, cast on 2 sts.

Knit 1 row.

Next row: Increase 1 st at each end of row (4 sts).

Repeat the last 2 rows four times (12 sts).

Work 2 rows.

Next row: Increase 1 st at each end of row (14 sts).

Repeat the last 3 rows four times (22 sts).

Work 16 rows without shaping.

Next row: K2tog, K to last 2 sts, k2tog (20 sts).

Work 3 rows.

Next row: K2tog, K to last 2 sts, k2tog (18 sts).

Repeat the last 4 rows six times (6 sts).

Bind off.

EARS

Cast on 3 sts.

Work 2 rows.

Next row: Increase 1 st at each end of row (5 sts).

Repeat the last 3 rows until there are 17 sts.

Work 2 rows without further shaping.

Bind off.

Make another 3 pieces.

TO MAKE UP NIGHTDRESS CASE

Sew the gusset between the two sides of the head, starting at the nose. Join the two side sections under the nose to the chin, leaving neck open. Stuff firmly. Close neck by sewing with running stitch and gathering the work; secure tightly. Embroider eyes, nose, mouth, and whisker features as

illustrated. Sew each pair of ear pieces together, then attach to head, gathering the wide edge slightly.

BAG

Lay out fabric, wrong side up, and fold a hem along each 27½ in. edge. Sew in place. With right sides together, put the newly hemmed edges together and sew, leaving an opening of approx 8–10 in. in the middle of the seam. Sew the bottom of the bag together, ensuring the open seam is in the middle of the bag (not on the side). Insert a lining at this stage if required, using the same method, securing it in each of the two bottom corners, and sewing together at the opening. Make a hem on the top of the bag and sew. Gather the whole top of the bag using running stitch, ensuring that the cat's head fits neatly into it. Baste the head in place, with the opening at the back, and sew. Add ribbon.

Bag with frilly top

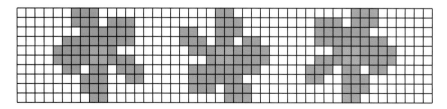

MATERIALS

- **Fingering yarn:**
  2 oz. white (A)
  2 oz. lilac (B)
  2 oz. muted green (C)
  2 oz. purple (D)
- Needles: size 3
- Double-pointed needles:
  size 3

BACK

Using yarn B (lilac), cast on 46 sts and work 2 rows in stocking stitch.
Change to yarn A (white) and work a further 2 rows in stocking stitch.
Continue working in this striped sequence until work measures 7 in.
Leave stitches on a stitch holder.

FRONT

Using yarn A (white), cast on 46 sts and work 4 rows in stocking stitch.
Following chart, complete the next 10 rows using both Fair Isle and intarsia techniques.
With RS facing and starting with a knit row, continue in stocking stitch until work measures 7 in.

Leave stitches on a stitch holder.

FRILLY TOP

With RS of panels facing, join one side seam using mattress stitch and slide all stitches on to one needle.
Using yarn D (purple), K 1 row.
Next row (WS): Inc in every stitch (184 sts).
Next row (RS): Starting with a knit row, work a further 4 rows in stocking stitch, forming the frilly edge.
Bind off.

TO MAKE UP BAG

Darn in all loose ends of motifs. Join side seam using mattress stitch.

HANDLES

Make two handles.
Using double-pointed needles and yarn C (muted green), cast on 5 sts. Knit 1 row * .

Without turning the work, slide the stitches across the left needle (from left to right), up to the point.
Bring the yarn across the back of the work from left to right and pull tightly. Knit the next row as before; repeat from * .
Continue until work measures 10 in. Darn in loose ends and sew securely to both sides of bag at the base of the frill.

□ A
 B
 C

Knitted bag

Knitted in brightly colored stripes and hearts, this little bag could be very useful for outings with Mom! The design uses only the most basic of knitting stitches, so it is an ideal project for beginners.

MATERIALS
- **Fingering yarn:**
  - 2 oz. muted green (A)
  - 2 oz. dark pink (B)
  - 2 oz. muted pink (C)
  - 2 oz. white (D)
- Needles: size 3
- Crochet hook: size C2–D3

TENSION
23 stitches, 32 rows
to 1 in.
Finished bag is 4 in. square.

MAIN BODY OF BAG
Cast on 46 sts.
Knit in stocking stitch throughout.
Follow Chart A for front and Chart B for back, setting motifs where desired.
When length of 4 in. has been

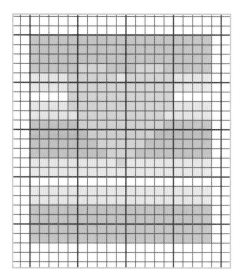

CHART A
Knitted in stripe sequence with green heart motif in intarsia.

CHART B
White background with two intarsia heart motifs.

□ **A**

□ **B**

C

□ **D**

□

knitted, knit one row of holes as follows:
K1, * yfwd, k2tog. Rep from * to end.
Continue in stocking stitch for 1 in.
Bind off.
To form picot edge, fold work at row of holes and slipstitch in place.

HANDLES
Cast on 12 sts.
Stocking stitch to length required.
Bind off.

TO MAKE UP BAG
Sew two bag pieces along sides and bottom, with picot edge at top. Sew handles to inside of the bag.

Yarn suppliers

Throughout the book, I have listed the general type of yarn that I recommend for knitting the various toys and accessories rather than a specific yarn. You can be a bit flexible about your yarn choices for a particular pattern: as long as the yarn you've chosen produces the required gauge, you'll get good results. Feel free to use different yarn textures and needle sizes for the projects in this book; doing so will you're your knitted toys personal and unique. Below are some suggestions for suppliers or companies who carry a wonderful range of yarn.

Fingering or Sock Yarn

Baby Cashmerino by Debbie Bliss
www.debbiebliss.freeserve.co.uk

Naturespun Wool or
Cotton Fine
by Brown Sheep
Brown Sheep Yarn Company
100662 Country Road 16
Mitchell, NE 69357
www.brownsheep.com

Baby Ull by Dale of Norway
Dale of Norway Inc., N16
W23390
Stoneridge Drive, Suite A
Waukesha, WI 53188
(262) 544-1996
www.dale.no

Babysoft, Jamie Baby & Jamie
Pompadour
by Lion Brand
Lion Brand Yarn Co.
34 West 15th Street
New York, NY 100011
(800) 258-9276
www.lionbrand.com

DK or Light Worsted Weight Yarns

Plymouth Encore DK
Plymouth Yarn Company
P.O. Box 28
Bristol, PA 19007
www.plymouthyarn.com

Provence by Classic Elite
Classic Elite Yarns
300 Jackson Street
Lowell, MA 01852
(800) 343-0308
www.classiceliteyarns.com

Kidsilk Haze by Rowan
Rowan Yarns
5 Northern Boulevard, Suite 3
Amherst, NH 03031
(800) 445-9276
www.knitrowan.com

Jo Sharp DK Wool
Jo Sharp Pty Ltd
CAN 056 596 439
P.O. Box 1018
Fremantle, WA 6959
Australia
www.josharp.com.au

Useful addresses & suppliers

Resources for other supplies, tools, and accessories

Stockade Craft Supply
www.stockade-supply.com

Karp Styles
9 Woodland Drive
Hay River, NT X0E 0R7
Canada
(867) 874-4657
www.karpstyles.com

A Child's Dream Come True
P.O. Box 163
Sandpoint, ID 83864
(800) 359-2906
www.achildsdream.com

All About Dolls
72 Lakeside Blvd.
Hopatcong, NJ 07843
(800) 645-3655
www.allaboutdolls.com

Doll Artist's Workshop
761 Quarter Circle
Gardnerville, NV 89410
www.minidolls.com

The Teddy Bear Making
Supplies Specialist
501 Gavilan Canyon
Ruidoso, NM 88345
(505) 336-2980
www.sparebear.com

Also available from Potter Craft:
The Knitted Teddy Bear
by Sandra Polley
ISBN: 1-4000-5437-0
$19.95
(Canada: $27.95)

Dozens of patterns that require
only basic skills for knitting your
own heirloom teddy bears,
clothing, and accessories.

Knitting abbreviations

k	knit	alt	alternate	tbl	through back of
p	purl	cont	continue		loop
st(s)	stitch(es)	patt	pattern	M1	make one stitch
inc	increas(e)(ing)	tog	together		by picking up
dec	decreas (e) (ing)	mm	millimeters		horizontal loop
st st	stockinette stitch	cm	centimeters		before next stitch
	(1 row k, 1 row p)	in	inch(es)		and knitting into
garter st	garter stitch (k	RS	right side		back of it
	every row)	WS	wrong side	yfwd	yarn forward
beg	begin(ning)	Sl 1	slip one stitch	yrn	yarn around
foll	following	psso	pass slipped stitch		needle
rem	remain(ing)		over	yon	yarn over needle
rev	revers(e) (ing)	p2sso	pass 2 slipped	cn	cable needle
rep	repeat		stitches over		

Needle sizes and conversions

Knitting needles are sized according to a standard sizing system, whatever material they are made from. There are three different systems: a metric system used in Europe and the UK; a US system; and an old UK and Canadian system.

Converting weights and lengths

oz = g x 0.0352
g = oz x 28.35
in. = cm x 0.3937
cm = in. x 2.54
yds = m x 0.9144
m = yds x 1.0936

Old UK & Metric size	US size	Canadian size
10	15	000
9	13	00
8	11	0
7½	10½	1
7	10½	2
6½	10½	3
6	10	4
5½	9	5
5	8	6
4½	7	7
4	6	8
3¼	5	9
3¼	4	10
3	2/3	11
2¾	2	12
2¼	1	13
2	0	14

Acknowledgments

Thank you to Mum for your endless support and countless hours of patient knitting and for teaching me the craft so many years ago, I will always be grateful. Thank you to Dad for my wonderful suppers and for the continual supply of tea. A huge thank you must go to all of my family and friends who encouraged me throughout this project and kept me going; I would not have been able to do it without you all!

I would like to thank Kate Buller at Rowan Yarns for supporting me over the years and thank you also to Rowan for supplying the beautiful yarns.

Thank you to Collins & Brown for the opportunity to make this book; I give particular thanks to Marie Clayton for her enthusiasm.

To all the ladies who have spent time with me and who have supported me at my workshops over the years, I thank you too!

My final words of gratitude must go to my partner Chris who has undeniably been a tower of strength throughout this long process. We can now go down the beach!